IMAGES
of America

VANDALIA
ILLINOIS

IMAGES
of America

VANDALIA
ILLINOIS

Brenda Baptist Protz

ARCADIA
PUBLISHING

Published by Arcadia Publishing
Charleston, South Carolina

Library of Congress Catalog Card Number: 00-107738

For all general information contact Arcadia Publishing at:
Telephone 843-853-2070
Fax 843-853-0044
E-mail sales@arcadiapublishing.com
For customer service and orders:
Toll-Free 1-888-313-2665

Visit us on the Internet at www.arcadiapublishing.com

Around 1916, a Murphy family photo was taken. In the front row, from left to right, are Charles A. Murphy Sr., Mary Barbour Murphy, Everett Murphy (a Vandalia policeman), and Charles "Albert" Murphy. In the back row, from left to right, are Ora Murphy, Ruby Murphy Stubbelfield, and Russell Murphy (father of local accountant Pat Gathe).

CONTENTS

Acknowledgments   6

Introduction   7

1.   Vandalia's Capitol   9

2.   Historic Downtown Vandalia   27

3.   Scenes Around Vandalia   51

4.   Vandalia's People   75

5.   A New Era in Vandalia   105

ACKNOWLEDGMENTS

There are not enough words to thank all of those who have in some way contributed to this book. Although I fear leaving someone out, I will attempt to name those who have helped me not only with this project, but those who have contributed to my other successes in life.

First, thanks to the following people who contributed to this book in various ways: Genelle Hachat; Jim Staff; Camilla Diveley; Hazel Jones; Wayne and Maija Deal; Delores and Ray Williams; Janet Shroyer; Beulah Brown; Charlie and Linda Townsend; Bret and Bunny Brosman; Charles Mills; Fleta Kistler; Mary Truitt and Nancy Stokes at the Fayette County Museum; Judy Baumann and staff at the Vandalia Statehouse; Glenda and Robert Young; First National Bank; Marcia Popp; Floyd and Lucile Bingaman; Sue Crawford; Jean Stombaugh; Jessie Maas; Denise Corbell; Pat Gathe; and Brian Stout. I especially thank Mary Truitt for her late-night rendezvous with me to help me collect pictures, and the Fayette County Museum for entrusting me with so many of their treasures. Of course, I must thank Steve Jerden, who scanned all of the photos, including the cover photo, to prevent the photos from being shipped out of town. Steve, thanks for doing everything you could to make this project a success.

And I couldn't miss the opportunity to thank all of those who have helped me throughout my life with words of encouragement, friendship, and love. First to my parents Frank and Barbara Baptist for their lifelong support and love; to my "other" parents, Jim and Glenna Mason, whose spirits guide me daily; to my brother Brian Baptist for teasing me; to my sisters Tammy Mason Rust and Lisa Mason Magelitz and their families for sharing their parents with me and for being my mentors for the past 29 years; to my in-laws Bill and Jackie Protz for helping, supporting, and babysitting; and to all of my family and friends who have ever supported me in my journalism.

Thanks also to the Vandalia Main Street Program for expanding my historical interest in Vandalia, and to my best friends at Mary Kay Cosmetics for encouraging me and giving me the tools to be successful. To my teachers in Jacksonville, including Beth Glenn, Margaret Johnson, Elizabeth Ahlquist, Roger Ezard, and Roger Zulauf; and to my college teachers in Springfield, including Mike Matulis, Mary Bohlen, and Hazel Rozema, THANKS!

And finally, I wouldn't be where I am today without my husband, Randy, and my daughter, Brandy, by my side. They sacrifice a lot for me to fulfill my dreams. And to my best friend, Jody McCurley, whose death at the age of 28 has prompted me to follow my heart and live each day as if it were my last. I thank you all.

INTRODUCTION

Growing up in Jacksonville, Illinois, as a child, I can remember visiting the Governor Joseph Duncan Mansion and hearing the stories of Governor Duncan making the long trek by horse to perform his duties as governor in Vandalia, then the state capital. I often wondered how that town of Vandalia came to be and how it was today.

In 1994, I was able to see for myself when my husband and I moved to Vandalia. I have had the opportunity to find out first hand about many of the people, places, and history that have made Vandalia the community it is today. While there are many historical books about Vandalia, including *Vandalia Remembered*, celebrating Vandalia's 175 years, and the *Souvenir Book of Vandalia*, from the early 1900s, this book, *Images of America: Vandalia, Illinois*, was designed not as a comprehensive history of the community, but as a sort of community scrapbook. It is a place for those people who had stories to tell and for those who had pictures that may have never been seen. But it was also a project for myself, an out-of-towner who wanted to learn a little more about this community that I now call home.

The city of Vandalia, and much of the rest of Fayette County, has been very good to me. In many ways, this is sort of a present to all of those who live here. It is important to remember that Vandalia really began in what is now our downtown area, so a lot of this book revolves around the downtown. And because the town began in this locale, I found it fitting to start the book there and to end it there. But the downtown area isn't the only thing that Vandalia is known for.

Many influences, such as the railroad system, helped to create Vandalia, and for the most part made downtown Vandalia what it is. The oil industry was very important, and it helped to improve the tax structure in the area. Additionally, other notable events occurred when Vandalia was the capital city. For example, Chicago received its formal city charter during that time.

Vandalia, however, is most known for its place in the beginning of Illinois politics. After the capital was moved from Kaskaskia to Vandalia in 1819, three capitol buildings were eventually built here. The first, located at 229 South Fifth Street, where the *Leader-Union* newspaper is today, burned down in 1823, under what Paul Strobel's book *High on the Okaw's Western Bank* describes as "mysterious circumstances." The second building was located on South Fourth Street, where today's Trail's End Saloon is located. This building was considered to be poorly built and was torn down in 1836. The current Vandalia Statehouse served as the state capitol from 1836–1839. And, during the time that Vandalia served as capital, a young, beardless Abraham Lincoln, from Sangamon County, came to town. Lincoln served in Vandalia as a representative from his county of Sangamon, and in 1837 made his first statement against slavery. It was also here that many political and other prominent figures lived, and in some cases, remained for life. Such sites in town as the Fayette County Museum, the Little Brick House, the Old State Cemetery, and of course the Vandalia Statehouse have been restored and preserved to show the city's place in history.

But this is also a town that wants to look towards the future. With growth on the north side of town increasing consistently, with quality factories, and with a revived commitment to improve the historic downtown area, the residents of Vandalia have shown that this is not only a community that is proud of its past, but one that knows what needs to happen to ensure a bright and prosperous future.

I hope that this look down memory lane is a pleasant one. And as I said previously, it can't possibly be a complete history, but a look back at some of the significant events that made Vandalia the place many were and are still happy to call home.

Pictured are author Brenda Protz, daughter Brandy Michelle, and husband Randy in 1997. The Protzes moved to Vandalia in 1994. Brenda has held positions at the *Leader-Union* and the Vandalia Main Street Program. Her husband became a math teacher and successful football and basketball coach at Vandalia High School beginning in the fall of 1994. Daughter Brandy was born January 18, 1996 to make the Vandalia family complete.

One

VANDALIA'S CAPITOL

Looking northwest from Gallatin Street, this is the Vandalia Statehouse early in the 1900s. Sections of the limestone slab walkway along Gallatin Street are still in use. The gazebo or "pagoda," pictured at the left, was often used as a bandstand or for other events. The pagoda was able to be moved on the grounds to suit a particular event.

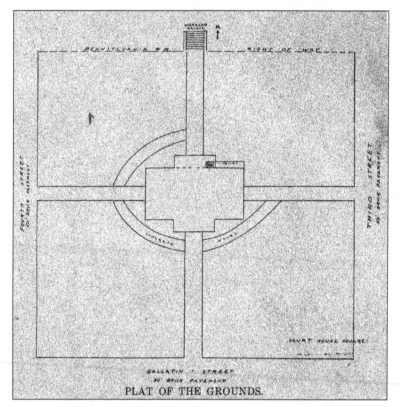

PLAT OF THE GROUNDS.

This is an original plat of the grounds where the Vandalia Statehouse is located. The plat was part of the 1918 Fayette County Bar Association and Board of Supervisors' Booklet.

This view of the Vandalia Statehouse, when it was known as the Fayette County Courthouse, was taken on April 1, 1913, and was part of the Fayette County Bar Association and Board of Supervisors' Booklet.

This historic photo was from 1911, when the building served as the Fayette County Courthouse. The people standing in the forefront of the statehouse are a good indicator of the overall massive size of the building.

This postcard features the Vandalia Statehouse when it was used as the Fayette County Courthouse.

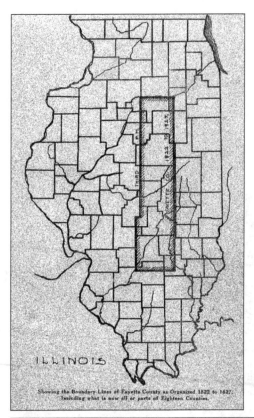

Showing the Boundary Lines of Fayette County as Organized 1822 to 1827, Including what is now all or parts of Eighteen Counties.

This map highlights the original Fayette County. Notice the boundaries for the county and how large Fayette County was originally.

This picture of the Vandalia Statehouse is from a postcard that was postmarked January 12, 1910, at a time when the statehouse was used as the Fayette County Courthouse. The postcard was sent from Avena to a Miss Leona Logue of Avena.

THE OLD CAPITOL, VANDALIA, ILL.

This photo of the south side of the Vandalia Statehouse, which shows the front door of the building, is from April 1, 1913 when the building was a county courthouse. The building was used in that capacity until 1933. The statehouse officially became a state historical site in 1940.

This west side view of the statehouse was taken on April 1, 1913. The statehouse at that time featured an iron fence, an early 20th century concrete walk, and hitching posts. In the left rear is the coal house.

This photo, showing the east side of the statehouse, is from April 1, 1913. This view shows the Charters Hotel in the background at left.

This is the only known photo of the interior of the Vandalia Statehouse when it was used as the Fayette County Courthouse. This photo is in the Circuit Clerk's Office. In the back left is Luther Staff, and a Mr. West is on the right. In the front, from left to right, are Mrs. West and Luther's wife, Ella Staff. Luther was the circuit clerk from November 22, 1912 until November 30, 1916. His grandson, James Staff of Vandalia, has continued in his grandfather's path of community work through his many years in the field of education and volunteer work in the Vandalia community.

The Vandalia Statehouse is shown here as it appeared between 1928 and 1940, with the *Madonna of the Trail* statue placed in front of the building. The statue was moved in 1940 to the southwest corner of the statehouse square so that the statehouse could be renovated to look as it did in the days when it was the state capitol.

Here is another view similar to the one above prior to 1940, when the Madonna statue was removed and replaced at the southwest corner of the grounds. This photo is from a postcard, which was a popular method of communication in those days.

This view of the front entrance of the Vandalia Statehouse was taken when it was used as the Fayette County Courthouse in the early 1900s.

On the second floor of the Vandalia Statehouse is the original wood flooring that was in place when the building was built in 1836. The flooring is the actual flooring that Abraham Lincoln walked on.

This is how the Capitol building looked in 1930. That same year the Vandalia Volunteer Fire Department kept the building from being destroyed by fire when sparks from the flue set fire to the cupola. The statehouse was painted red at that time.

In March 1930, when the Vandalia Statehouse was the Fayette County Courthouse, the fire which started as the result of sparks from the flue setting fire to the cupola was photographed. This is the only known photo of the building on fire. The fire did an estimated $18,000 in damage, but as was reported in the book *Vandalia Remembered*, Circuit Clerk Fred G.W. Easterday managed to get his office cleaned and opened by the following Monday morning.

This image of the statehouse was taken sometime between 1941 and 1945. The Vandalia Lions Club was the sponsor of the Honor Roll Board. In the years it stayed on the lawn of the statehouse, the board had more than two thousand names of World War II servicemen added from Fayette County.

This aerial view of the downtown area was taken about 1943. The statehouse and the other downtown properties have changed since then, but the area continues to be a popular place for tourists and local citizens in 2000.

In December 1986, this photo was taken just after the building was re-painted and a wooden fence and new sidewalks had been completed. A handicap ramp and roof repair were also completed.

Judy Baumann, site superintendent at the Vandalia Statehouse for the Illinois Historic Preservation Agency, is shown here giving tourists a demonstration during a guided tour of the building. Baumann has been site superintendent since 1988. The first superintendent of the property was Kathryn Tedrick Brooks. It was through the hard work of Brooks that the Grand Levee celebration began, and it was under her that the statehouse became a site that the state took more of an interest in restoring.

This is the desk of Governor Reynolds, the fourth governor of the state, which is featured inside the Vandalia Statehouse. This is an original piece from the second capitol in Vandalia, which was located at the site of today's Trail's End Saloon, just west of the current statehouse on Fourth Street.

Shown is one of the original wood-burning furnaces in the Vandalia Statehouse. The stove is a J.V.R. Hunter Sally Ann with a Sunburst pattern. There are two original stoves in the building that have been there since 1836 when the statehouse was built.

This desk, in the House of Representatives' Room in the Vandalia Statehouse, is an original piece from the time the building was used as a capitol. It was in this room that Abraham Lincoln spoke out against slavery, and it was also the place where Stephen A. Douglas served. Douglas was a representative here from Morgan County, and Lincoln was a representative from Sangamon County.

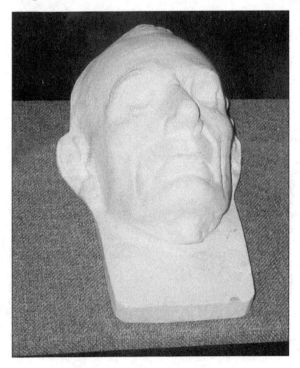

The Vandalia Statehouse is also home to a replica of the original life mask of Abraham Lincoln that was made by Leonard W. Volk in March 1860. The Evans Public Library is also home to one of the replicas, as well as several other pieces of Lincoln-era historical documents, pictures, and books.

In recent years, the downtown area surrounding the statehouse has been used for many special events. In this photo a car show, sponsored by Watson's Saw Shop in cooperation with Vandalia Police Department's DARE Program, was held during the 1999 Fall Festival. The drag racing cars pictured are owned by Randy Protz of Vandalia.

In 1999 improvements began on the Vandalia Statehouse. The exterior was tuckpointed, the wood trim was replaced, and a new copper roof was added. The work continued into the year 2000 when this phase of renovations was completed.

Here is the statehouse in 2000 after completion of improvements to the exterior. A major renovation is planned in 2001 that will include a new mechanical and electrical system, and new exterior walkways will be installed made of brick. The office of the site superintendent will be moved from the first floor to the basement. An employee break room and a storage room will also be placed in the basement.

Two

HISTORIC DOWNTOWN VANDALIA

This late 1800s photograph shows downtown Gallatin Street. This photo shows a downtown parade. In later years, Vandalia has become known for its parades, especially during Halloween festivities.

This photo from the early 1900s shows a sale taking place at the James Evans and Sons Hardware Store, located on the north side of Gallatin Street. The sign on the storefront says "Charter Oak Range Sale." There is also a group of men standing above the group, who appear to be attempting to get a rise out of the crowd. It should be noted that this is now the site of the First Bank Building and drive-up area

The Hotel Evans was built on the site at Gallatin and Fourth Streets, which once was the site of the Charters Hotel. The five-story structure had 100 rooms, of which 65 had bathrooms. The hotel featured an elevator and free parking. Built in 1924, it was destroyed by fire in 1969. The hotel was built by Charles A. Evans, and featured the Abe Lincoln Cafe as well as the "Blue Room," an exclusive blue dining room. The hotel was recognized by tourists as the finest hotel in southern Illinois.

The Eakin Hotel was referred to as Vandalia's first fireproof hotel, and was built by William Eakin around the time of the Depression in the 1930s and 1940s. The former hotel today is owned by the First Baptist Church. The church uses the hotel as rental apartments. At left is the Eakin Garage, which is now known as "The Way Inn," and is used by the church for various activities.

The W.E. Fogler Furniture Store is pictured here in the early 1900s. The site was also known as the Jacob Fouke building, and was built in 1891. The storefront boasts the items that were sold. On the left window are the words "Furniture and Carpets." On the right are the words "Coffins and Caskets." The building, located at 416 West Gallatin, is currently the home of the Nice Twice Resale Shop, and for many years was "The Model" clothing store.

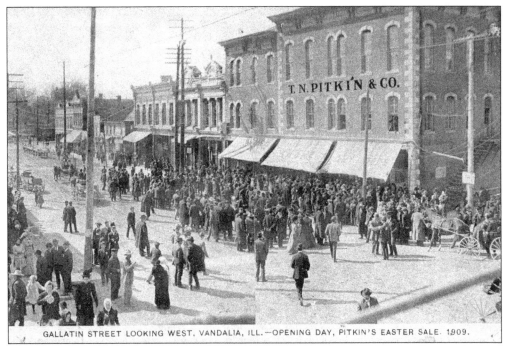

GALLATIN STREET LOOKING WEST, VANDALIA, ILL.—OPENING DAY, PITKIN'S EASTER SALE. 1909.

This photo is from about 1907. This was the opening day of the big T.N. Pitkin Easter sale. Men and women alike appear to have come to find the big bargains. Later, this corner became the site of Polk Atkinson's General Store. This is now the site of the China Gate Restaurant and Something Special Florist.

This early 1900s view of Gallatin Street is of what appears to be an Old Settlers Parade. The building on the right is the Dieckmann Hotel, now the First National Bank. Notice the balconies on the Dieckmann, allowing people to stand and watch the parade.

From 1909, this photograph shows Gallatin Street looking east from the top of Lutheran Hill. The archways across the streets were an interesting feature then, and were on each end of Gallatin Street. The railroad tracks also went across Gallatin Street at that time.

This postcard view of Gallatin Street was from about 1910. Notice that there is only one visible car and several horses and wagons. Light poles have been added and the period lighting is in the place that the City of Vandalia is trying to once again bring to the downtown. This view is looking west with the Charters Hotel on the right.

This is another view of Gallatin Street on the north side. There are visible light poles which tell us that the photo was taken in the late 1800s.

The T.N. Pitkin & Co. building at the corner of Fifth and Gallatin Streets was a very successful business in the early 1900s. The building, which now houses the China Gate Restaurant and part of Something Special Florist, was taken over by T.N. Pitkin in 1890, after many other successful businesses had been located there. The Pitkin family home on South Seventh Street is now the home of Greg and Renee Philpot and family.

A view from the late 1800s shows the building at the northeast corner of Fifth and Gallatin Streets. The building has been known as the Easterday Building, and in more recent years was the Piggy Bank Pawn Shop. The building has been vacant and deteriorating for several years, but will hopefully be rejuvenated rather than demolished.

This was a scene from Gallatin Street around 1916 or 1917, when Company I left Vandalia. They had been training for WW I. A big parade was held to celebrate the many Fayette County soldiers who were leaving.

The offices of Gochenour Insurance were located on the southwest corner of Fifth and Gallatin, now the site of McKellar, Robertson, and McCarty Insurance. The company was organized in 1867 and merged with the Dycus Insurance Agency in 1985, which was founded in 1942. Mike Hall is the present owner of the merged Dycus and Gochenour Insurance Agency, located at 319 West Main. The big building in the center was the Aaragon Hotel, which contained Burnett's Restaurant.

This photo is from a float which appeared in the 1938 Old Settlers Parade. There were more than one hundred schools represented in the parade, which became an annual tradition during the duration of the Old Settlers events. Pictured in the background of this photo is Fidelity Clothiers, Humphrey's Drug Store, and the Morris Dime Store.

Barber shops were a popular spot for not only getting a hair cut, but for catching up on the town gossip, and in this shop, even getting a hot shower. This was the Deal Barber Shop, owned by Tony Deal, which was located on Gallatin Street in the general location of Maranatha's Tips & Clips today. Those cutting hair are, from left to right, Tony Deal, Roll Deal, and Van Sears. The fourth barber is unknown. The barber shop was at that location from the early 1900s through the 1920s.

This picture of Fourth Street looking north shows that horses and wagons were once a common sight in downtown Vandalia. This view, taken in the late 1800s, shows the Charters Hotel at the left. This block now is home to Giuseppe's Pizza, Discount Tobacco Inc., Trail's End Saloon, Timmerman & Company Ltd. CPAs, Schauffelberger and Bauer Law Office, and Atchley's Glass Service.

According to the book *Vandalia Remembered*, this photo shows Vandalia's volunteer fireman cleaning the streets. Many businesses once occupied the area that is now the First National Bank parking lot.

This photo must have been taken before the *Madonna of the Trail* statute was moved to its current location in 1940. It shows Fourth Street and the Evans Hotel at left, before it burned in 1969.

Shown is a photo of Gallatin at Fourth Street, probably taken from the Vandalia Statehouse cupola. The large building in the center is today Cuppy's Old Fashioned Soda Fountain and Hallmark. At right is Charters Hotel, where it is believed Abraham Lincoln stayed the night while a young politician in Vandalia. At the left is the building once occupied by the Denny's Dept. Store and later Allen's Furniture.

The Charters Hotel was located at the corner of Gallatin and Fourth Streets, now the site of Giuseppe's, a favorite pizza restaurant. The hotel was on what was referred to as Hausmann Corner, and was considered a fine hotel during the time Vandalia was the state capital through 1839. As of 1904, the property was considered an eyesore, was torn down, and later became the home of the Evans Hotel.

This view is from inside the Ebenezer Capps Store located at the corner of Fourth and Main Streets. The store featured hardware, school supplies, pharmaceuticals, and grocery items. Capps was born in London, England in 1798 and settled in Vandalia around 1829. He died in 1877, and the business was carried on by his sons Charles and George. The business was torn down in May 1910.

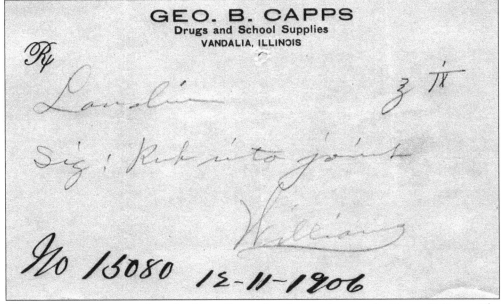

This is a prescription paper from the Capps Store when it was taken over by George B. Capps. The prescription is dated December 11, 1906, and was for Lanolin. The signature says "Williams."

The Dieckmann Hotel was a popular hotel that was built with the most modern amenities. This photo was from a postcard that is addressed to Marshall L. Wilson of Vandalia and has the message "Merry Christmas and Happy New Year to you, from George A.A. Dieckmann." The hotel, which was built in the 1800s by August H. Dieckmann, was later owned by August's nephew, George A.A. Dieckmann. George had renovated it by January 1, 1905. There were 45 sleeping rooms, and the completed hotel and furnishings cost in excess of $55,000.

The hotel lobby of the Dieckmann Hotel was an inviting place for those coming to stay. The hotel, which is now the First National Bank, was renovated by George A.A. Dieckmann and contained all of the most modern amenities.

This postcard features the Dieckmann Hotel. The Dieckmann Hotel was frequently photographed, especially for the purpose of postcards. This postcard features the First National Bank on the lower level.

Shown is an advertisement poster advertising the Dieckmann Hotel's meal hours. The dining room was described as "beautiful, large and light" in the 1904 *Vandalia Historical Souvenir* book.

MEAL HOURS
=AT=

The Dieckmann
Vandalia, Illinois.

Week Day.			Sunday.		
Breakfast	-	6.15 to 8.30	Breakfast	-	7.00 to 9.30
Dinner	-	11 45 to 1.30	Dinner	-	12.30 to 2.00
Supper	-	5.45 to 7.30	Supper	-	6.00 to 7.30

Guests Please Notice.

This is the card room inside the Dieckmann Hotel. The hotel had many interesting features like the card room, which was probably very popular among the gentlemen.

The dining room inside the Dieckmann Hotel was a favorite spot as well. Breakfast, dinner, and supper were served there after the hotel was reconstructed and improved by W.A. Lucas, a well-known St. Louis architect. The hotel featured modern conveniences, including hot and cold water.

This 1940s postcard view shows Gallatin Street looking west. At the right is the Evans Hotel, which is now Giuseppe's. At the left is Fidelity Clothiers, which is now Cuppy's Antique Soda Fountain.

HUMPHREY'S DRUG AND BOOK STORE,
VANDALIA, ILLINOIS.

For ....

Rx 25 ds Worth, 1/2 gr Sulphide
of Calcium Tablets—
Take one 4 Times
a day
147726
9-26-06   Dr Greer

Shown is a prescription written by Dr. Greer on September 11, 1906. The prescription was taken to Humphrey's Drug and Book Store, which was in the site now occupied by Cuppy's. Otto Cuppy would later carry on the drugstore tradition, opening up Cuppy's Pharmacy in 1969.

This view inside the First National Bank is from 1909. Pictured, from left to right, are Cashier Robert H. Sturgess, President William M. Fogler, and Joe Easterday, who would later become the president of Ramsey National Bank.

This is another view of Fifth Street behind the then Dieckmann Hotel. A feed store, restaurant, and other stores were in what is now the parking lot for the First National Bank's loyal customers.

This was one of Vandalia's two depots from the late 1880s. Vandalia has a rich history in the railroad system. Vandalia's initial investment in the railroad was reported to be about $49,000. Many historic events occurred here through the railroad, including the November 21, 1915 passing through of the Liberty Bell, and also the funeral train of President Dwight D. Eisenhower.

This is Vandalia's only surviving depot. This depot was constructed and completed by October 11, 1923, and was considered to be one of the finest depots in Illinois. In the 1930s, passenger service was discontinued in Vandalia. The current owners of the depot are Debra Hamel and her brother, Doug Gates, who purchased the building in 1996. After many hours of renovation, they have created a unique dining experience, and were careful to preserve many of the historic features of the depot. Named simply "The Depot," the restaurant's property is completed by the bright red caboose which was brought in and renovated in 2000.

"Stombaugh's"   Vandalia Ill.   1954

This photo of Stombaugh's, when it was located on South Fourth Street where Timmerman's is today, shows Glen Stombaugh inside the business. The date on the photo is 1954. Glen was the second generation to run the business, which specialized in heating and air conditioning. His father, Thomas, began the business in 1911, and it was later run by Glen's son, George. George's son, Steve, is the fourth generation to run the business. Its current location is 329 South First.

The current owners of this home at 628 West Gallatin are Bret and Bunny Brosman. The Brosmans purchased the home in 1990, and have spent the past ten years restoring the home to its former prestige. Built in 1895, it is a Queen Anne Victorian home that was built by M.F. Houston. M.F. Houston married Lydia Snyder, and although they lived on Gallatin Street, they also had a farm on Route 40, called Waverly Farm, which is now owned by Wayne and Maija Deal. Mr. Houston owned a hardware store, and his name can even be seen within the stained glass inside St. James Lutheran Church. Current owner Bunny Brosman said they began renovations on the home when they moved in, and that it has been a constant work in progress.

In 1961, Jane Isbell began the jewelry store in its current location at 414 W. Gallatin. The store merged with Day's Jewelry in 1969. Prior to the jewelry business, Isbell worked from 1944–1961 at the F.F. Burns Drugstore, which was located east of the First National Bank Main Building. Shown in the photo, from left to right, are Kathryn Jones, Mary Humphrey, Jane Isbell, Pat Reavis, and watchmaker Ed Ruescher.

This photo shows a more modern view of the south side of Gallatin Street across from the Vandalia Statehouse. At left is Old Capitol Antiques, and the building at center and right is Allen's Furniture Co. The furniture store has been in operation for more than 65 years, and the current owners are Lorraine and Rita Mae Allen. The current building was purchased in 1936.

This view of the interior of Burtschi Brothers Title and Abstract Company shows the original safe in the center of the building. The safe was part of the original Commercial Bank started in 1910 by Julius and Joseph C. Burtschi.

The Burtschi family officially began the business in 1894 when Julius and Joseph C. Burtschi issued their first insurance policy. The business currently is owned by Patsy Schutz, who took it over in 1987.

Three

SCENES AROUND VANDALIA

This postcard from 1976 shows the Mabry Court Motel, which was another popular motel in Vandalia. The motel was located behind the current Jays Inn Restaurant and featured 72 sleeping units, a swimming pool, color cable television, and shuffleboard. The motel currently serves as rental apartments and office spaces.

The Ford Roofing Products Company was in Vandalia from the early 1900s until about 1950. The company, which was located on West Main Street, employed between two hundred and four hundred people during its times of production.

This is a postcard featuring the Kaskaskia River Bridge at the foot of Gallatin Street in about 1904. At the bottom is the steam yacht of E.B. Spurgeon and Harry J. White.

One of the first public pools in Vandalia is shown here.

This photo shows the interior of the F.F. Burns Drugstore and soda fountain. The store featured Hydrox ice cream, and pictured at right are some of the many cosmetics that were sold. The store was located east of the First National Bank Main Building where their addition sits next to Victoria's Fashions.

Old National Road Bridge over Okaw River, Vandalia, Ill.   1244 HAND COLORED   ROBT E MITCHELL PUB

This view of the Old National Road Bridge over the Okaw River is from a unique hand-colored postcard. The postcard was sent to a Miss Emma Molz in Pana on August 27, 1908.

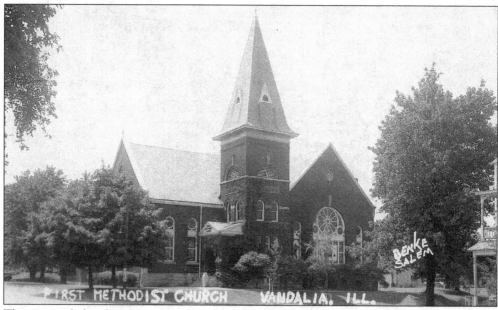

FIRST METHODIST CHURCH   VANDALIA, ILL.

This postcard, dated May 9, 1950, shows the First United Methodist Church on Fourth Street. The postcard was originally sent to a Raymond G. Bradley of Collinsville, Connecticut, and the message reads "Having a swell time 1022 miles away from home, Fred."

Known as "The Waverly Farm," this home located on Route 40 in Vandalia has been in the Deal family since 1937. The home's current residents are Wayne and Maija Deal, who moved into the home in September 1999. The 160-year-old home was the summer residence of George F. Houston. The farm was settled by George's grandfather, Augustus Snyder, in 1840. This home was also used as a Girl Scout Camp site in the 1920s. Around 1927, many local Girl Scouts, including Hazel Crawford Jones, attended camp here and camped out on the front porch of the home and studied nature.

The American Legion Home is shown here on a postcard. The building was originally the M. Fehren Mansion, which the Legion purchased in 1943. It was renovated by 1946 when WW II veterans were coming home. The north-side addition was later completed in 1986.

The Robbins Motel and Restaurant was a popular restaurant and motel located at what is now the corner of Eighth and Veterans, where the new Sonic Drive-In is located. Owned at this time by Mr. and Mrs. Cloyd Nevinger, the motel featured 33 rooms.

56

This postcard dated 1913 shows the First Baptist Church, located at the northwest corner of Sixth and Johnson Streets. The church was organized in 1894 and boasts a large congregation. Its services are recorded for a television broadcast.

The Mother of Dolors Catholic Church was featured on a postcard complete with a 1¢ stamp. The first Catholic mass was conducted in Vandalia by the Rev. George A. Hamilton of Springfield on May 11, 1845, at the Fayette County Courthouse, only six years after it had ceased being the state capitol. The current church is located at 322 North Seventh and was dedicated on May 21, 1898.

The St. James Evangelical Lutheran Church, located at Eighth and Gallatin Streets, was completed in October of 1869. The church was constructed at the site that came to be known as "Lutheran Hill," after another location on Main Street was abandoned as a church.

This photo is believed to be an early photo of the First Presbyterian Church, now the Fayette County Museum, located at the corner of Main Street and Kennedy Blvd. The church was erected in 1866, and the first service was held in the basement in December of 1866. This photo is probably from the late 1800s.

This is the First Christian Church as it has appeared in recent years, which is located at the northwest corner of Randolph and Fifth Streets. The church was begun in March 1923, and was dedicated in February of 1926.

East Bound Train on the Vandalia Line, Vandalia, Ill.   1242

This postcard dated July 30, 1914, shows the east-bound train on the Vandalia Line. The postcard was addressed to Mrs. Lillian Walker, who apparently was in the hospital in St. Louis. The sender, Lillie, wrote "Dear Lillian, Hope you will soon be speeding home in an auto like the one on the front of this card."

The Evans Youth Center, a log cabin, is located at the corner of West Randolph and Eighth Streets, and was donated to Vandalia by Mr. and Mrs. Charles Evans in 1940. The Boy Scouts and Girl Scouts use the building, as well as other youth-related groups.

The Vandalia Country Club appeared this way before being destroyed by a tornado on July 15, 1955. The Vandalia Country and Golf Club organized in 1915, and is now in its second building, celebrating the 85th anniversary of the club.

The Don Jones Studio at the corner of Seventh and Johnson Streets, which is now the Regional Office of Education, was newly constructed in the 1950s. The photographic studio featured two camera rooms, including the one shown in the background offering a modern portrait camera. The studio was designed by its owners, Don and Hazel Jones, who also are responsible for starting such businesses as The Village Shoppe and The Sunshine House Health Food Store, both of which are still flourishing. Other notable photographers have included Browning, McLeod, Bob Thoman, and now Voegele Photography.

The old county jail, shown here, was demolished in 1968. Its former plot is now the location of the Fayette County Soil and Water Conservation District and the Illinois Department of Human Services, behind, or east of, the post office. The sheriff at the time this photo was taken in the mid-1960s was W. David Brown, husband of Beulah Brown. Beulah said her husband originated the idea of building the first jail at the courthouse.

This is the kitchen inside the old jail. Neta Kelly was the primary cook at the jail, and would be replaced by the sheriff's wife, Beulah Brown, when she wasn't available.

This is a jail cell in the mid-1960s in the old county jail. Notice that on the wall to the right is a calendar, which the inmate must have looked at frequently until his release.

Here is the office inside the old jail in the mid-1960s. The desk chair was normally sat in by Sheriff W. David Brown, but at times was used by a dispatcher. The sheriff's deputy, Leonard Kelly, and wife Neta, lived in the jail. The sheriff's wife, Beulah, recalls voters telling her husband that they wouldn't vote for him if he moved his family into that jail. For the record, Beulah states, "We never lived in that jail."

The Johnson, Stephens, and Shinkle Shoe Factory was a major industry in Vandalia, and employed two hundred workers in 1924. The number of employees had increased to six hundred in 1949 when the company celebrated its 25th anniversary. According to Charles Mills in the book *Vandalia Remembered*, the factory produced Rhythm Step women's shoes and made about 2,500 pairs of shoes each day. For many years, the company also made shoes for the New York City Radio City Rockettes. The company closed in the 1970s due to foreign competition.

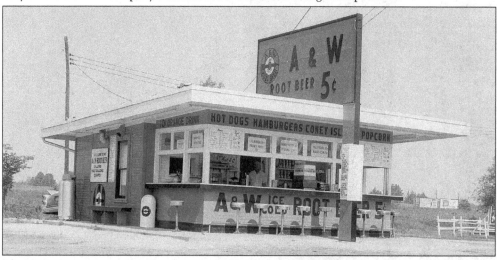

The A & W was a popular root beer stand and was located where Dr. Joe Moore has his Tri-County Medical Clinic today. Erma and Elmer Hachat ran the store first in 1955, and then sold it to Helen and Melvin Donnelley. Elmer then bought it back around 1959 and ran it until July of 1969. The Hachat's daughter, Genelle, said that Marjorie and John Blythe bought it from her parents. Genelle has many fond memories of growing up in the A & W, and also said that the location at one time hosted a taco restaurant.

Back in the 1940s, the Toot'n Tell'm was a popular north end eating spot and hang-out for both young and old. The woman pictured is waitress Wanda McCollum. The restaurant was located at the northwest corner of Seventh and Orchard Streets.

This is a close-up of the Dairy Queen with a sign saying "See You Next Spring." The Dairy Queen then, as it does now, closed during the winter months.

Next door to the A & W on Eighth Street was the Dairy Queen, owned by Jim and Ada Chandler. Dairy Queen's face has changed a little, and a drive-through has been added, but current owner Pauline Deverick still serves the best ice cream around. Pauline, along with her late husband, Charlie, has owned Dairy Queen for more than 30 years.

This image shows the Vandalia Municipal Water Softener and Purification Plant. The plant was put into operation on December 15, 1951. At the time the plant had a daily capacity of one million gallons of water per day, and today it has a capacity of 1.6 million gallons per day. On average, Vandalia residents use about 900,000 gallons per day.

Postcards were a very popular means of correspondence before telephones and e-mail came into play. This postcard features the old Vandalia High School.

This photo shows the initial construction phase of the Vandalia Lake in 1966. The man in the photo could be an employee of Harre Construction of Brownstown, which was initially the company that cleared the property.

Here is another view of the beginnings of the Vandalia Lake in 1966. The project resulted in an area which now boasts many lake camping sites, a beach, and lakefront property featuring some of the most beautiful homes in Vandalia.

This giant flag was constructed by the late V.A. Kelley along Interstate 70. The flag was one of many of Kelley's roadside attractions, including a miniature church which Kelley constructed for travelers. Kelley was famous for his outspokenness and was even a candidate for president of the United States. The property along the interstate was sold in the late 1990s after Kelley's death.

This photo shows the interior of the downtown Sears location. The store opened in the late 1960s and closed in 1990. Ray and Delores Williams owned the store from 1984–1989. It was located at 300 West Gallatin where Donaldson's Carpet is today.

The Beau-Meade House, located at 606 North Sixth Street, became Vandalia's first bed & breakfast in 1999. Owned by Robert "Chris" and Glenda Young, the home is thought to have been built by George Kurtz Sr. during the Civil War.

This 60-foot replica of the St. Louis Arch was built by Harry Mabry in 1965. Mabry designed the arch and had it placed in front of the Travelodge Motel, which he owned at that time. The arch, now 35 years old, continues to be a popular attraction for those passing through Vandalia.

This photo of the old Standard Oil Products station at Third and Gallatin Streets was taken around 1938. The station's site in later years was known as JR's Phillips 66 at the corner of Gallatin and Kennedy Boulevard. The Standard station was owned by Harry Bingham for many years, and later by Harold Moyer.

This bridge originally was located near the corner of Johnson and Fifth Streets, and provided a passage over the Illinois Central Railroad on Johnson Street. The bridge was near the *Leader-Union* newspaper and was torn out in 1988.

Four

VANDALIA'S PEOPLE

This photo was from one of the local Rotary Club's celebrations from the mid-1950s. Pictured, from left to right, are as follows: Frank M. Denny; Dr. C.D. Washburn, dentist; Harold Newton; and Charles Evans, owner of Evans Hotel. The club was organized in 1925 and celebrated its 75th anniversary in 2000.

Pictured are some of the staff members from the former Denny's Clothing Store. They are, from left to right, Dave Reeter, Iola Sears, Frank Denny, Wave Eller, and Vernon Berger.

In this photo from April of 1965, a ribbon cutting was being held at the First United Methodist Church for the new education building and fellowship hall. The education building has been used for many years for many church-related and community events.

William Deems, then the administrator of the Fayette County Hospital, was honored in about 1951 for not only his birthday, but for pioneering many of the hospitals in Illinois. It was reported that during Deems' tenure at FCH, the hospital had equipment that wasn't available even in St. Louis. The cake that is being cut was made by Lenora Stonebrunner Kern and looked like the hospital with marshmallows for windows. Pictured, from left to right, are as follows: Camilla Diveley; Earl Crabtree; Clem VanZandt; Dr. A.R. Whitefort; Dr. Miller Greer; Rosemary Deems; Reavis Brown, local band director and mortician; William Deems; Dr. E.P. Staff; Dr. Glen Walker (partially hidden); Sylvia Bouchez, Director of Nursing at Fayette County Hospital; and Cleolla Pope, Director of Housekeeping.

Dr. Mark Greer, a long-time physician and philanthropist in Vandalia, as well as the person who started up the first hospital in town, was honored for being named the Doctor of the Year for the State of Illinois. Pictured, from left to right, are Dr. Greer's wife, Iris Greer, Dr. Greer, and at far right is Mildred Hackleman. Dr. Greer was born in Vandalia in 1889. Under his direction, a hospital was established in 1925 at the site where Dr. Brian Dossett's offices are now. The Fayette County Hospital was built in 1953 due to the continued support of Dr. Greer and the community. Dr. and Mrs. Greer were also known for deeding the land to the Vandalia School District for the building of the new Vandalia Community High School. The building was completed in 1950, and the athletic field was named in his honor.

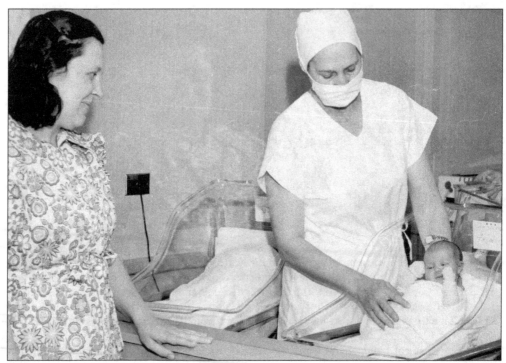

Here is a picture inside the nursery of Fayette County Hospital. Pictured is nurse Olga Studenberg, who was supervisor of the OB Department. The baby she is holding up has the name Thompson behind its head. The photo is from the mid-1950s.

Bill Runyon, a retired Pennsylvania Railroad employee, was known for his annual portrayal of Santa Claus during the 1950s. Here he is pictured giving a wave to passersby from a Pennsylvania Railroad engine.

This large group gathered around 1954 to pose for a group photo of the Pentecostal Church Bible School. Churches around Vandalia continue to offer Vacation Bible Schools to young people in the summer months.

Camilla Diveley was heard over the airways for many years through WCRA of Effingham. Diveley would read the local news from the First National Bank lobby and did so for many years. The 19-year run of the news program was begun in the 1940s by Vodithe Diveley Reavis, and continued by Camilla. The program featured local news, hospital reports, and area news. Camilla would turn her love for the media into a lifelong passion. She wrote a column for the *Centralia Sentinel* newspaper from 1956 to about 1980, and was also a freelance reporter for WCRA in Effingham as well as the Associated Press and the United Press International.

A feature of the First National Bank was the giving of flower seeds to customers. The customers would then grow the seeds and bring the flowers into the bank for judging. Presenting the awards were Harry Rogier, bank president; and, from left to right, Irene Fink, unknown, Margaret Torkelson, Vivian Carson Schmid, and Camilla Diveley, who helped with the program.

The Hudson Dairy on West Gallatin is shown here in the early 1920s. Shown in the photo are Raymond Tevis, at left, Claude Largent, in the center, and other unknown men. On the wall is a sign that reads "Please Do Not Ask For Credit."

The Water Works Department in Vandalia is shown here installing a new pump on July 30, 1902. Pictured, from left to right, are Ky Manion, "Mr. Golden Insurance Agent," Joseph Rummel, David Schert (top, at right of pole), Joseph Leach (below Schert), Mr. Metcalf, Joseph Smith, Mayor George Steinhauer, Charles Stimson, Mike Brannon, and William Oliver. This information was printed on the photo, but it is also possible that this could be the electrical power plant.

A group of Vandalia residents assembled around 1915 for a photo on the steps of the Evans residence, now the site of the Evans Public Library. In the front row, the couple at the right is Mr. and Mrs. Myron Harding, grandparents of Don Jones and great-grandparents of Jeff Jones and Jan Jones Stover.

Many groups have used the Vandalia Statehouse as a backdrop for photos. Here, a group of men posed in the early 1900s.

This is the second grade class of Central School on October 9, 1924. In the front row, from left to right, are Elaine Bost, Marjorie Bell Moore, Marcella Etcheson, and Hazel Crawford. In the second row are Gerald Moore, Richard Hamilton, Gene Hawk, Tom Stombaugh, and William Pross. In the third row are Mary Reed, Pauline Dieckmann, Lucille Gerkin, Pearl Richards, Gwynette Carter, Jean Hood, and Edith Crotser. In the final row are teacher Fern Goad, John Frakes, Arnold Jones, Robert Cole, Lynell Guinn, Floyd Largent, Jack Lauderdale, and Robert Schaffer.

The *Vandalia Union* newspaper owners and staff had a staff photo taken in 1914. In the front row, seated, from left to right, are Margaret Torkelson and Flossie Bradley. In the back are K B. Mills, owner Ira Lakin, owner Jess Lakin, and Norman Jones. K B. Mills would later own the *Vandalia Leader*.

Vandalia's enterprising Jones family was photographed in 1956. In the front is then-owner and operator of the *Vandalia Union* newspaper Norman Jones, his wife Bess Jones, and their daughter, Mary Jean. In the back row are sons Don, Ken, and Fred.

In 1958 the Charles Crawford family posed for their family portrait. At one time, all four of the Crawford children owned and operated businesses in the downtown area. Pictured in the front row are father Charles Crawford, daughter Ina Mae Crawford Eadie, who along with husband Bill operated Eadies Bakery, and mother Fannie Crawford. In back is son Stanley Crawford, who ran a restaurant and ice cream parlor; Hazel Crawford Jones, who with husband Don operated Don Jones Photography; and Ken Crawford, who ran a grocery store and restaurant. In 2000, daughter Hazel Jones was inducted into the Senior Illinoisans Hall of Fame at a ceremony held at the Illinois State Fair. Jones was lauded for having an impact on Vandalia's labor force for more than 65 years. Jones can be credited with starting up current businesses such as The Sunshine House Health Food Store, The Village Shoppe, and The Senior Review, as well as the former Don Jones Studio with her husband. She has also co-hosted a morning radio show with daughter Jan.

Fannie Crawford, standing at right, was featured in the September 4, 1952 issue of *The Cosmetic News*, a newsletter for Fuller's Debutante Cosmetics dealers. Fannie began selling the cosmetics in 1948 and reported that in two years she had 121 parties and made well over $2 an hour. This photo shows a group of Vandalia women practicing makeup application. In the photo, from left to right, are Alberta Smith Wooten, Norma Smith, Grace Grider, Mary Grider, Francis Lingle, Trudy Thompson, and daughter Hazel Crawford Jones.

In 1937, this curly-headed blonde was photographed playing with her kitten. The child, Kay Sue Eadie Nagle, is the daughter of Ina and Bill Eadie who owned and operated Eadies Bakery on Gallatin Street for many years.

The day was December 17, 1954, when local photographer Don Jones brought his then 3-year-old son, Jeff, to the lobby of Mark Greer Hospital at the corner of Eighth and Jackson Streets, to visit his mother, Hazel, and 2-day-old sister, Jan. Notice the Christmas tree in the background decorated in the hospital lobby. This photo marked the first of many times that Jan and Jeff Jones would be photographed for a Christmas card.

This photo was taken in the early 1900s. The photo shows Lucy A. Brown, center, the widow of Civil War soldier James H. Brown, with their children, their children's spouses, and grandchildren. The family photo was taken as part of an "Old Settler's" celebration. At the far left, seated with a beard, is O.L. Brown.

A special memento was printed in observance of the 60th wedding anniversary of Mr. and Mrs. Hector Humphrey. The Humphreys, who were married May 22, 1851, were very prominent in the community. Hector was the founder and ex-editor of the *Vandalia Union* and a former postmaster. The Humphreys lived at the corner of First and Madison Streets.

MR. AND MRS. H. S. HUMPHREY

CELEBRATION OF THE 60TH ANNIVERSARY OF THEIR MARRIAGE, MAY 22, 1911,

This photo of the Vandalia Municipal Band is believed to have been taken in 1936. Ray Williams was a tuba player in the band. The statehouse appears in the background before it was renovated and the bigger columns were added.

Sister and brother Jan and Jeff Jones pose as Christmas carolers for their family's Christmas cards in about 1957. Their parents, local photographers Don and Hazel Jones, photographed and processed the family Christmas cards that were sent to customers, family, and friends.

The officers of the Fayette County Courthouse look happy to be posing for this photo in about 1936. Seated behind the desk is Sheriff Charles Brannon. Sitting to the left is Bob Burnside, then the Fayette County State's Attorney. Seated at right is Superintendent of Schools Kenneth Greer. In the back is Circuit Clerk LaVerne Deal, Judge Charles Myers, Deputy Sheriff Dennis Brown, County Clerk Glen Curry, and County Treasurer Ray Robbins.

These three women ran the Don Jones Studio while their husbands were serving in World War II from 1943–1945. Pictured, from left to right, are Hazel (Don) Jones, who served as photographer and colorist; Rosalie (Allen) Wirz, who was the receptionist; and Kathryn (Fred) Jones, who worked in the darkroom.

This photo was taken by the Don Jones Studio. In the photo at left is Orlando Lorenzo (O.L.) Brown, who was then the president of Vandalia Mutual Insurance Co. At right is W.E. Miller, who was secretary. Vandalia Mutual Insurance exists today on Gallatin Street and is combined with Willms and Yakel Insurance. Notice in this photo that the First National Bank calendar is from 1939, and the small calendar reads that the date is April 8.

Don and Hazel Jones, owners and operators of Don Jones Studio and Camera Shop, started their downtown studio in 1938 and later branched out into several other businesses in town. This photo was actually being taken by Don Jones while he and Hazel posed. Don's right hand was actually holding the bulb, enabling him to take the picture of himself and Hazel.

James Henry Brown of Vandalia served in the COB 42nd Illinois Infantry. He was born in 1824 and died in 1864 while fighting for the Union Army in the Civil War. He was the grandfather of Fleta Kistler, now of Loogootee.

The widow of James Henry Brown, Lucy Ann Sarah Brown, was born in 1829 and died in 1906. After her husband was killed she was left to take care of their large family.

At left is Lawrence LaVerne Deal with his new bride, Irma Lucille Ley Deal. The couple were married on September 18, 1929 in Metropolis. Irma was a 1925 graduate of Vandalia High School, and was a bookkeeper at the Old Capitol Creamery. Deal graduated from Vandalia High School in 1927 and was the manager of the Deal Tonsorial Parlor on Gallatin Street. He later would be a Fayette County Circuit Clerk. Their home, known as the Waverly Farm, is on route 40, and is still in the family. Son Wayne and his wife Maija Deal are the current residents.

In the late 1800s the law firm of Farmer and Brown was changed to Brown, Burnside, and Bullington after Judge William Farmer mentored James G Burnside and Josiah T. Bullington and they passed the bar exam. Pictured at left is John J. Brown. At third from left is James G. Burnside.

John J. (J.J.) Brown was admitted to practice law around 1876. Brown started his life as an orphan from New York City but ended up living in Bear Grove Township with a farmer named William Henninger. Brown would later form the Farmer and Brown Law Firm with William Farmer. That original merger later became today's law office of Burnside, Johnston, and Choisser. Brown died in 1932 after having been an ex-member of the legislature, and running for the office of Secretary of State.

The other half of Farmer and Brown Law Firm was William Farmer. Farmer was born in 1853 in Pope Township in Fayette County. Farmer graduated from law school at Union College (now Northwestern University) and was admitted to the bar in 1876. He and J.J. Brown formed their partnership in 1883, and their office was located on the second floor of 330 West Gallatin, which is now Allen's Furniture. Farmer would later become the Circuit Judge of the Fourth Judicial Circuit, and he served 25 years as a judge on the Illinois Supreme Court. He died in 1931.

The first basketball team at Vandalia High School is pictured here in 1906. Pictured in the front row, from left to right, are Alvin Hudson and Joe Easterday. In the middle are Clare Cox, Ben Perkins, Howard Davis, and Homer Frailey. In the back row are Mark Greer, Harry Leever, Coach A.M. Newton, Charles Smith, William Rethorn, and Harry Tate.

Harry Rogier, seated at the desk, was the president of First National Bank from 1944–1966. He is pictured here with bank employee Barb Shanafelt, at left, and WCRA radio announcer Camilla Diveley. The three were discussing the radio program that Diveley announced and First National Bank sponsored.

The employees of the Denny's Clothing Store celebrated Christmas in 1953. In the front row, from left to right, are Margaret Balsinger, Eva Bowles, Rollin Porter, owner Frank M. Denny, Wave Eller, Camilla Diveley, and Mary Isbell. In the back row are Wayne Braye, Hugh Jerden, Mary Force, Joan Simpson, Claude Schellabarger, Martha Bowles, Iola Sears, Estella Frank, Earlee Fry, and Eldon Autenrieth.

The annual Jaycees Home Show always drew a crowd and showcased area businesses and products. This photo shows the mass of people who came out in 1962. Radio station WPMB/WKRV would later hold the home show in the gymnasiums of the high school and middle school, but stopped holding the event in 1999.

Vandalia High School has produced an annual yearbook to celebrate the activities and students each school year. Pictured at left is yearbook editor Judith Davis and yearbook advisor and teacher Helen Barr, who also is credited with starting the homecoming celebration at the high school in 1946. Barr taught at Vandalia High School from 1945 to 1979.

This photo of the Vandalia Fire Department was taken in August of 1942. Since the volunteer fire department's inception, its members have assisted at thousands of fires, including the one in 1930 that saved the Vandalia Statehouse from being destroyed. In the year 2000, Merle Adermann serves the department as chief.

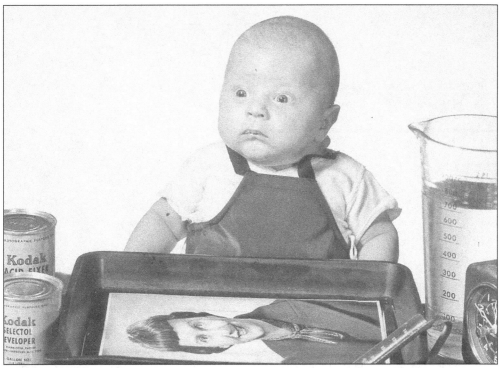

In 1951, 2-month-old Jeff Jones was propped up for this special photo. Jeff, who is wearing a miniature photographer's apron, a baby gift, appears surprised that the picture he is developing is that of his mom, Hazel Jones. Jeff's father Don took the picture.

Pictured later are Jeff Jones and his wife, Deb, in 1984 when they purchased the store from his parents, Hazel and Don Jones, who had owned the store since 1976. In 2001, the store will be celebrating its 25th anniversary.

The Coonskin Band was a popular band in the 1920s and played frequently at the local Moose Lodge. Standing are Herman Troike, Selby Cheshier, and Tony Deal. Seated are "Dock" Boaz, Gus Bruckner, and Wayne "Banjo" Brown. The photo was taken by Browning Studios in Vandalia.

This photo contains five generations of the Deal family. The photo appeared in the *St. Louis Post-Dispatch* on September 21, 1930. Pictured, from left to right, are LaVerne Deal, 23; his father Tony Deal, 45; LaVerne's son Wayne, 17 months old; LaVerne's grandmother, Mary Deal, 66, of St. Elmo; and LaVerne's great-grandmother, Mary Phillips of Cowden. At the time, baby Wayne had ten living grandparents. This photo also appeared in the *Decatur Herald & Review*, and that newspaper reported that Tony Deal was its first Vandalia subscriber.

This souvenir card was from the Old Settler's "School Day" on September 10, 1937. Many prominent educators were present when this photo was taken in front of the Vandalia Statehouse.

SOUVENIR

OLD SETTLERS "SCHOOL DAY" AT VANDALIA

------September 10, 1937------

SOME PROMINENT EDUCATORS PRESENT

LEFT TO RIGHT: E. B. Tucker, superintendent of Effingham county schools; Otis Keeler, assistant state superintendent of public instruction; Mrs. Cora B. Ryman, Decatur, superintendent of Macon county schools; John A. Wieland, state superintendent of public instruction; O. F. Patterson, assistant state superintendent of public instruction; G. Kenneth Greer, Fayette county superintendent of schools; F. E. Crawford, Vandalia, former Fayette county superintendent of schools; Representative C. F. Easterday, Vandalia, former Fayette county superintendent of schools; Paul B. Chance, Salem, superintendent of the Marion county schools; and S. B. Vance, former Fayette county superintendent of schools.

Jim Staff has always been very active in Vandalia athletics and in the education process. Here he is shown with the Central School Basketball Team of 1954–1955. Pictured in the front row, from left to right, are John Harris, Charles Cocagne, Ronald Hourigan, Mike Waltz, Gary Towler, Tom Bowles, Tom Tate, Tom Cocagne, and Roger Harting. In the second row are Charles Manion, Charles Eadie, Jim Parsons, Mike Brannon, Jack Parker, Kippy Dugan, Ralston (Buzzie) Edwards, Jim Wickersham, Jim McLaughlin, Jerry Brock-Jones, Max Qualye, and Ed Enriquez. In the third row are William P. Schultz, Bruce Bannister, John Royal, Ronald Koehler, Sherrell Horsley, Lowell Rinehart, Joe Landes, David Burtschi, Steve Kuehn, Tom Spurlin, and James F. Staff. In the fourth row are Bill Clark, Jim Hulskotter, David Crawford, George Stabler, Jerry Branham, Eldon Perry, Douglas Eadie, Joe Wright, and Bill Hunter. In the fifth row are Keith Carr, Ronald Deutsch, Jerry Lockart, Jerry Parsons, Fred Garland, Ed Salisbury, Jim Bowen, Gary Kirkman, and Larry Henna. Not present for the photo were Tom Greer, Paul Holaday, John Lipsey, and Gene Hamilton.

In 1969, a 37-year-old Otto Cuppy opened up the doors to Cuppy's Pharmacy. Since that time his business expanded to include Cuppy's Hallmark and Gifts, Cuppy's Old-Fashioned Soda Fountain, and Cuppy's Antique Mall. He has since retired from the pharmaceutical business, and the old pharmacy has now been replaced with the antique mall, but Otto Cuppy will be known for his common sense and his "let's just get things done" approach to everything, in addition to his dedication to the downtown area.

In 1960, Vicki Nutter was chosen as Miss Vandalia at the third annual Jaycees Home Show. That summer she was chosen as Miss Illinois and went on to compete in the Miss America pageant. Here, she is being welcomed back to Vandalia by State's Attorney Martin Corbell and Mayor Cecil Smith.

The Vandalia Volunteer Fire Department was first organized in 1862. Records later show that the Vandalia Fire Company was organized on October 15, 1889. This picture is from the early 1900s.

The fire department shows off a new fire truck. Pictured in the early 1950s are Harold Hartwick, at left; Verle Laswell, in the truck; Clarence Smith; and Phil Craycroft, at right.

This photo from the early 1900s is of the Vandalia Municipal Band. The photo, now owned by Marcia Brown Popp of Edwardsville, shows Popp's grandfather, Fred L. Brown, seated in the first row at left. Fred was the son of A.L. Brown of Vernon, and the grandson of James Henry Brown, a farmer from Wilberton Township who was killed in the Civil War. O.L. Brown was his uncle.

At left is Fred Brown; his son, Glenwood, is on the right. They are pictured in front of the *Madonna of the Trail* statue after marching in a Vandalia parade in the 1930s. Fred Brown had his own band from the age of 16, and ordered all of his instruments from New York and also taught many friends to play music. In 1930 he organized 40 elite musicians to form the American Legion Band with N.O. Harris serving as the director. Glenwood was also a band director who originated the marching band at Bradley University in Peoria. He was also the director of the Peoria Municipal Band until his death in 1945.

Fleta Pearl Brown is shown on July 16, 1911. Fleta was the youngest of 12 children and is the only surviving member of the O.L. Brown family.

This is Fleta Pearl Brown Kistler today. She married John Israel Kistler on January 18, 1930. They had one son, Rex, who lives in Vandalia.

This is the headstone for Ferdinand Ernst, one of the original German settlers in Vandalia. Ernst was a German agriculturalist who brought a group of Germans to Vandalia in 1820 after the town was made the state's capital in 1819. His grave is located in the Old State Cemetery on Edwards Street.

The grave of Colonel Robert Blackwell is also in the Old State Cemetery. Blackwell came to Vandalia at the very beginning and spent his entire life in Vandalia. He was best known as being the first auditor and public printer in the state of Illinois. He was born in 1796 and died in 1866. He was a part of a large group of prominent citizens in that time.

104

Five

A New Era For Vandalia

The Village Shoppe is one of the very successful businesses in downtown Vandalia. Owned by Virginia Mabry, the business is known for its gift baskets and for its gourmet coffee. Mabry and her staff pride themselves on customer service, as well as their quality gifts. Mabry made renovations to her building in 1999 and 2000 to renovate the upstairs and create a unique apartment for her granddaughter, Cassie Biellier.

This is Robert "Chris" and Glenda Young. The Youngs have been well known in the Vandalia community for dressing up at local events as Uncle Sam and as "Mrs. Sam," as she is commonly referred to. The Youngs traveled to the Illinois State Fair in 1999 and had their picture taken with the Uncle Sam-decorated cow, part of an exhibit at the fair called "Cows on Parade."

This view of the north side of Gallatin Street in 2000 shows, from left to right, Burtschi Brothers, H & R Block, Vandalia Mutual Insurance Agency/Willms and Yakel Insurance Agency, T&T Hobby, and, hidden on the far right corner, Giuseppe's Pizza.

Bill LaDage, long-time educator and volunteer in Vandalia, and Tim Summers, a former teacher and current volunteer and coach, helped the Vandalia Main Street Program in September 1999 by being the emcees for the first annual Farmers' Appreciation Day. The event was organized to show support for the Vandalia area farmers and featured a petting zoo, farm-related games, a dunking booth, music, and other fun events. The event was to be repeated on September 23, 2000.

In 2000, the First National Bank celebrated 135 years in downtown Vandalia. The bank's location was once the site of the Dieckmann Hotel, and although it has undergone much renovation since the Dieckmann days, the nostalgia surrounding the building can still be felt. The bank features a collection of old bank mementos as well as old photographs from the days when it was the Dieckmann. Ernie Chappell is currently president of the bank.

This photo was taken in August 2000, and features the inside of Cuppy's Old-Fashioned Soda Fountain in downtown Vandalia. Owned by Otto and Peg Cuppy, the store features the soda fountain, a Hallmark Gold Crown Store, an antique mall, and, new in 2000, a store called Melanie's Candles and Crafts owned by Robert and Gaby Hamilton. The restaurant has become a popular place in the downtown to have lunch and ice cream, and especially to have a bite of Nori Pruitt's famous lasagna.

The exterior of the Cuppy's Building is shown here in 2000. The building, which formerly housed many other successful businesses including Humphrey's, Fidelity Clothiers, and First National Bank, is one of the most popular places in the downtown. The building, which was placed up for sale in 2000, has been in the Cuppy family since the late 1960s.

Located at 516 West Gallatin, Cain's Drug Store features not only prescriptions, but a fine line of gifts as well. Here are employee Diane Rebbe and co-owner Bonnie Tjaden. Bonnie, along with husband Darryl, has owned and operated the pharmacy downtown since April 1, 1985. The original Cain's has been in business since 1937 in the same location.

On March 30, 2000, former United States Senator Paul Simon came to the Vandalia American Legion to help with a fund-raising event for the Vandalia Main Street Program. Simon, now Director of Public Policy at Southern Illinois University at Carbondale, came to Vandalia to help with the original fund raiser for the Main Street Program's life-size, bronze statue of Abraham Lincoln. With Simon in this photograph is Sue Donaldson, a former home economics teacher at Vandalia High School and a faithful community volunteer.

This is another modern view of Gallatin Street. At this site is the Nice Twice Shop at the far left, the Sunshine House Health Food Store in the middle, and Victoria's Fashions on the right.

This mural of Abraham Lincoln will serve as the backdrop for the Vandalia Main Street Program's Lincoln Park. The park, which is located in an empty business lot, was originally designed by landscape architect Katherine Brown and further refined by Main Street volunteers. The park will contain a gazebo, fountain, flowers and trees, and a life-sized bronze statue of Abraham Lincoln. The park is scheduled to be completed by the summer of 2001.

The members of the Vandalia Vandals Wrestling Team became the state champions in 1996. The 1990s saw much success in Coach Glenn Exton's teams, and they brought home the first team state championship trophy in the history of Vandalia Community High School athletics.

Here is the interior of the Nice Twice Shop in downtown Vandalia. The resale shop is staffed by volunteer workers and is sponsored by the Lutheran Child & Family Services. The store provides reduced rate clothing, toys, and household items and has been a valuable way of helping others in the community.

1997 IHSA STATE
WRESTLING TOURNAMENT
CLASS A

Nathan Graumenz was named a state wrestling champion in 1997 in the 135-pound weight class when he claimed an individual title. Graumenz was a part of a successful reign of Vandalia's wrestling teams, and was also a part of an extended Graumenz family who made significant contributions to Vandalia Community High School athletic programs for many years. Nathan became the third individual in Vandalia to win an individual state championship. Larry Staff won the state championship in the shot put in 1952. Richard Rames would later be state champion in the high jump in 1975.

From a downtown parade in 2000, Mayor Sandra Leidner rides in a 1960 red Corvette convertible driven by Mark Miller. Leidner became the first female mayor in Vandalia in 1997 and will run for reelection in 2001. Leidner is also a long-time educator in Vandalia, and is currently a teacher at the Vandalia Middle School. Mark Miller is a mortician with Miller Funeral Homes.

Vandalia's very own Lewis "Abe" Clymer has represented Vandalia for many years as Abraham Lincoln. Clymer, who owns Clymer's Television and Appliance downtown, is part of the Association of Lincoln Presenters, an organization that he succeeded in convincing to hold their 2002 annual meeting in Vandalia. Pictured here with "Abe" are Leigh Wieda and her daughter Jaclyn Ralston in 1999.

This is one of the newest fire engines owned and operated by the Vandalia Volunteer Fire Department. The engine was purchased in 1996 from LTI of Ephrata, Pennsylvania.

The Vandalia Statehouse is the home of many activities throughout the year. In 1999 the statehouse held its annual candlelight tour and gave away ornaments to the first one hundred people on December 11. Here, Mary Truitt greets a group of Boy Scouts as they enter the statehouse.

The Fayette County Museum, formerly the First Presbyterian Church, is shown as it appears in August 2000. The museum volunteers designed the Colonel Robert K. McLaughlin Historic Garden in 1999, situated just west of the museum. Colonel McLaughlin was the first treasurer in the state and moved to Vandalia when it became the capital. McLaughlin was married to Isabella, who was the niece of Shadrach Bond, the first governor of Illinois. The McLaughlin's home was on the site of the new garden. The brick walkway of the garden features the names of many Vandalia area residents who donated to the park and museum.

The big bear that was located at the entrance of Cuppy's Old-Fashioned Soda Fountain and Hallmark Store was a fixture at Cuppy's since about 1993. The bear was a gift to Otto Cuppy from his wife, Peg. The bear was frequently dressed by employees for various occasions. Here he is shown dressed for the July 4, 2000 holiday. The bear was sold to a bear collector from Sherman in September 2000.

Here, the bear, dressed as Santa Claus during Christmas of 1999, is shown with 3-year-old Brandy Michelle Protz. Brandy is the daughter of Brenda and Randy Protz, and loved to visit the bear whenever she came to Cuppy's. Another popular fixture among the kids at Cuppy's is the old-fashioned, claw-foot bathtub displayed in the store that has held everything from giant gorilla stuffed toys to hundreds of Beanie Babies.

This shows the interior of Victoria's Fashions during the Christmas season of 1999. The store was established in downtown Vandalia by Vicki Ellsworth in September 1997, and current owner Bonnie Sampson took over ownership in October of 1999. The store features women's clothing, bridal and formal dresses, and accessories.

This covered wagon has become the symbol for the National Road Association of Illinois. Through this organization, the National Road officially received scenic byway status in the year 2000. The National Road, also referred to as the Cumberland Trail, was the first roadway system that stretched between Cumberland, Maryland and the Ohio River. The road would later become U.S. 40 in the 1920s. Vandalia is the terminus of this road, as money ran out before it could be extended.

This photo shows the Christmas room of Something Special Florist, owned since 1983 by Donelle Conaway. The store features fresh and silk flower arrangements as well as other gifts. Big sellers at the store include memorial flowers and Christmas items. In 1999, Donelle organized the "Santa's Cottage" across the street and decorated the interior of the former Bo-K Flowers building to house Santa and Mrs. Claus during the holiday season.

A group of local residents took to the microphones to sing at the first Farmer's Appreciation Day in 1999 sponsored by the Vandalia Main Street Program. The event was a success and brought many people downtown. Pictured, from left to right, are Connie Bolyard, Main Street Chairman Bill Donaldson, City Administrator Ron Neibert, Beverly Hood, Joy Oldfield, and Billye Marquardt.

In 1999, Santa and Mrs. Claus came to town for the first time the Saturday after Thanksgiving in November. The Clauses were escorted into town in one of the horse and carriage combinations owned by Bob's Legacy Carriage Company in Beecher City. The Clauses enjoyed their temporary home, "Santa's Cottage," which was headquartered in the former Bo-K Florist building. Santa and Mrs. Claus are holiday favorites portrayed by Jerry McDowell and Rowena Biellier.

Several members of the Baroque Folk performed in March 2000 for the Abraham Lincoln statue fund raiser held at the American Legion. Pictured, from left to right, are Dorothy Ann Jenkins, Lisette Ehrat, and Dee Donley. The Baroque Folk play period music on recorders and entertain at many area events, including the Grand Levee, a period celebration held annually at the statehouse during Father's Day weekend.

Santa meets the Indian in this photo at Christmas, 1999. The Santa, portrayed by Frank Baptist of Jacksonville, and father of Brenda Protz, is shown with the famous Gallatin Street Indian which is in the front yard of the home owned by Bret and Bunny Brosman. The Indian is carved out of an old elm tree and is still attached at the roots. Carved by Mike Sugg with some help from Bret in 1991, the Indian has become a popular attraction on Gallatin Street. Bunny Brosman reports that it's not unusual to look out her window and see tourists in her front yard having their pictures taken with the giant Indian.

The *Madonna of the Trail* statue was placed in Vandalia on October 28, 1928, and was moved to its current location in 1940. The statue pays tribute to the pioneer women who made the trek down the Cumberland Trail with their families. The statue is one of several that appear throughout the United States along the Cumberland Trail. The statue was erected by the National Society of the Daughters of the American Revolution to mark the national trails traveled in this country's early years.

This photo from 1985 shows the Industrial Expansion Photo Day held in downtown Vandalia. The photo was to be used to market Vandalia industrially and drew much publicity world wide. The photo contained several thousand people and served as an idea for other communities around the state to have their own town family portraits. The photo was taken by local photographer Bob Thoman.

Taken in the Vandalia Statehouse on December 11, 1999, the Executive Board of the downtown revitalization group, The Vandalia Main Street Program, looks on as Board President Bill Donaldson signs the agreement between the organization and artist John McClarey of Decatur. McClarey was commissioned to sculpt a bronze, life-sized, seated Lincoln statue to be placed in the program's future Lincoln Park, located across the street from the statehouse. Pictured, from left to right, are Gwen Johnston, Joy Oldfield, Rodes Hood, John McClarey, Bill Donaldson, Brenda Protz, Jean Stombaugh (partially hidden), Sandy Peyton, and Otto Cuppy.

At the March 30, 2000 Abraham Lincoln statue fund-raising event held at the American Legion, Bea Cearlock, left, and Gene Cearlock, right, were the high bidders for the miniature Abraham Lincoln statues. The Cearlocks purchased *Signature Series Maquette #1* for $2,600. Pictured with the Cearlocks is the sculptor, John McClarey of Decatur. At the event ten statues were auctioned off and one was raffled, raising more than $14,000 for the program.

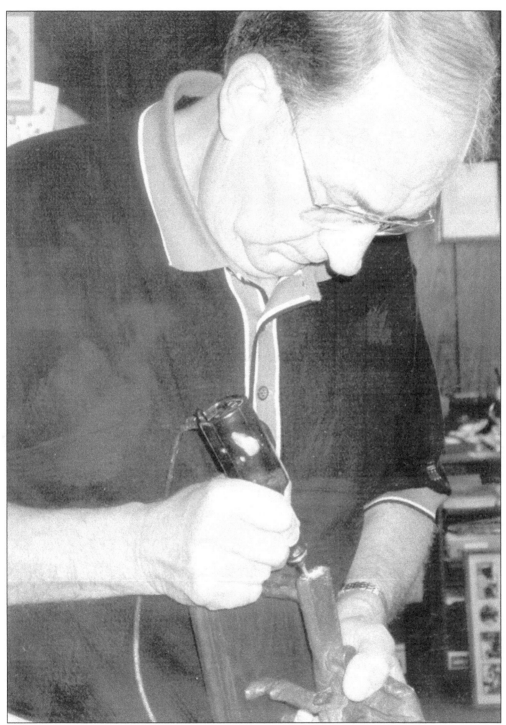

John McClarey of Decatur, designer and sculptor for the Vandalia Main Street's "Sitting With Lincoln" statue project, makes some finishing touches on a miniature statue. Only one hundred of the statues were created by the artist and area residents were a part of a lottery to see if they were chosen to receive one and pay $250 for each statue.

This photo of the first Vandalia statue shows how many people turned out for the dedication of the *Madonna of the Trail* in October of 1928. The event was a grand affair which included a

ASSN AND VANDALIA C OFC VANDALIA ILL OCT 24 1936

parade and around 10,000 spectators. The event, which was held on the lawn of the Vandalia Statehouse, is also the captured in the photo which appears on the cover of this book.

A close-up of a larger version of the Abraham Lincoln statue was on display at the Vandalia Statehouse in 2000. A life-sized version will also be created by John McClarey and will be placed in its location across from the statehouse in February of 2001, in time for Abraham Lincoln's February 12 birthday. The statue, along with the *Madonna of the Trail* statue, is expected to be a big tourist attraction and is part of the Illinois Heritage Tourism project of "Looking For Lincoln."